M000036067

Soulwhisperings

Erotic And Devotional
Love Poems
For An
Outer Or Inner
Beloved

Tina M. Benson, M.A.

Copyright 2016 ~ Tina M. Benson, M.A.
All Rights Reserved

Cover Image Courtesy:
J.P. Singhal Foundation
Website: www.jpsinghal.com

Cover Design by:
Ag Ario Kusumo
diztrix666@yahoo.co.id
Instagram: ARIOSTIGMAKUSUMO

ISBN-13: 978-0692773451
ISBN-10: 0692773452
Library of Congress Control
Number: 2016914115
Satya Books, Mill Valley, CA

FOREWARD
BY ALFRED K. LAMOTTE

(All in italics are from the poems by
Tina Benson)

As the author of three books of poems, all of them about the path of mystical love, I was drawn to Tina Benson's work, as she was drawn to mine. We became friends because our hearts irradiated one another, even when we lived far apart in the illusion of material distance. I invite you too to discover your proximity to Tina's heart, through these poems that burn away what seems to separate our souls.

Many intuitives in this age are re-awakening the Way of the Heart, and poetry is often the vessel that carries this nectar of awakening. Not a new way, this is the path of the Christian mystics, Sufis like Rumi and Hafiz, Medieval troubadours, ecstatic poet saints of India like Mirabai and Lalladev. From diverse cultures and religions, these mystic poets all share a common language, at once sensual and transcendent, to express the inexpressible joys and losses of Love's work in the human heart.

Erotic language is the only vocabulary for putting this inner fire into words. The Eros of mystical love means weeping as well as joy. It means getting lost in the dark, where we are penetrated by that beam of light that impregnates our soul with a splendor that cannot be likened to anything but the rapture of the nuptial bed.

Tina Benson's poems invite us to consider the possibility that, within the bridal chamber of our own chest, we can make love to God. This ecstatic union demands a language of transcendental sensuality. Here, as in the greatest mystical poetry, every voluptuous image of earthly love points to an interior rapture for those who are doing soul-work.

> *I want your fiery breath*
> *on my belly,*
> *your sound in my ears,*
> *your salt in my mouth*

Do these words speak of the dance of two bodies in love, or the communion of soul and Spirit through the breath of meditation, the sound of the mantra, the ecstatic taste of the Divine Name?

God is not a theological abstraction in these hymns, but an active lover, more intimate to the psyche than the psyche to herself:

> *Fertilizing me,*
> *impregnating me*
> *with your breath!*

As every meditator knows, the mystery of union can be realized through the most primal human act: breathing. What could be more physical, more immediate? Simple respiration becomes a silent prayer, and in the purest communion, we receive our very inhalation as the gift of the Beloved. So this poet cries for us all: *I want your fiery breath!*

Tina's best-selling first book, "*A Woman Unto Herself: A Different Kind of Love Story,*" was a woman's discovery that the love she thought would come through a man's external form, was the ecstasy of her own divinely human Self-radiance. Yet the journey to wholeness involved terrible pangs of transformation and purgation. Mystics know well that the way of loss is the only path to fullness.

In this second book, Tina gives us a song cycle that we may read as a number of interlocking poems, or a single hymn of ecstasy. Her song of songs begins with the recognition that:

> *There is an aching in the human soul*
> *for Holy Communion*
> *with ourselves...*

The path from that ache of longing, to the recognition that we ache for our own beloved Self, is a burning path, a nameless way, a wayless pathless surrender. For only the loss of who we are not, acquaints us with who we are.

Tina begins, as do all true mystics, by inviting us to become naked, to strip ourselves of the false identities with whom we masked ourselves, because we sought love in the wrong places. Her poem cries:

> *Undress yourself.*
> *Stand unveiled.*
> *There is no other way to touch God.*

Tina invites you even to *leave your name outside.* The soul who abandons herself for love's sake may even feel at times that she is losing her mind:

Where is the asylum
For lovers gone mad
With the intoxication of Love?

Yet in the end, it is a blessing to lose this mind! Why should the lover not want to lose a mind so full of doubt and fear, chattering with the past and future, when the Beloved is pure Presence?!

Yes, only through loss can we find, in Tina's words: *the unfathomable love that one Is.* Self-loss is a purification that cleanses the heart and prepares the marriage bed. This song-cycle takes the reader through the entire spiritual path: from purification to ecstasy, from apophatic mysticism (emptiness without images) to cataphatic mysticism (fullness of the divine Beloved).

In the end, these poems offer triumph – triumph that is inward and quiet, yet more solid and lasting than any external reward; the triumph of brave lovers who burn away the darkness through the power of Self-luminosity. Tina Benson's poems reveal that in love, we find eternal light: *We are ablaze in our own incomprehensible beauty.*

~Alfred K. LaMotte

Alfred K. LaMotte is the author of two books of poems published by Saint Julian Press: *Wounded Bud: Poems for Meditation,* and *Savor Eternity One Moment At A Time.* He is co-author of an art book, *Shimmering Birthless: A Confluence of Verse and Image,* published by artist Rashani Réa. LaMotte is a college instructor in Philosophy and World Religions, and an interfaith chaplain.

For Lovers Everywhere

Part One

Love Poems

Life is so sensual...

Had I known

How sweet

Your nectar would be

I'd have starved myself

A thousand lifetimes

For just one drop

Where is the asylum

For lovers gone mad

With the intoxication of
Love?

Admit me now

So I may howl at the
moon freely

With the rest of the
crazies

Let me run naked

In all this madness

Surely all the lunatics
there will understand

There is an aching

In the human soul

For Holy Communion

With ourselves

With each other

With life itself

Allow it

Undress yourself

And stand unveiled

There is no other way

To touch God

LOVE itself

Has become my Guru

*There is nothing I need
to know*

*That it doesn't have to
teach me*

*You are my Holy
Communion*

My Beloved

Your sweet ambrosia

*My only wafer and
sweet wine*

The moment the
fertilized egg

Begins to divide

Spiritual hunger

Is born

To return

To the seed

Of our original
Wholeness

The Temple lives

Inside the eyes

Come in

Pray

Sing

Dance

Chant

But leave your name

Outside

It is not your riches or gold

That interests me

I want your fiery breath

On my belly

Your sounds

In my ears

Your salt

In my mouth

Something burns

In my chest

Aching to find words

To give meaning

To the Yearning

This yearning

This holy, holy
yearning

It wakes me

In the middle of the
night

Feverish to fall into

The center of things

Continued...

Like Mirabai, lost

Consumed by a passion

For a lover

She is already

In consummation with

How can one yearn
most

For what one is already
burning with?

How can the flame that
licks me clean

Burn any hotter?

I have gone mad

With the drunkenness
of this fever

Oh God...I'm on my
knees

Don't save me now

*In the moonlit secret
chambers of my heart*

*There is a riotous dance
of celebration going on*

It is only when I behold
myself

And you

As beautiful

And filled

With as much mystery

As a rose

That I am seeing

With clear eyes

For we have come here

As nothing but beauty
and love

And it is to love

We are always
returning

I could go the ashram

To pray at your feet

Or I could worship you

In every breath

With each offering

Of my love and
devotion

To those around me

Every day

When the time comes

Oh Lord

For me to take my last
breath

Here in this grand
mystery of life

I pray the word that
has lingered

the longest upon my
lips be

"YES!"

We who are lovers

We recognize each
other

If even in beggar's
clothing

Through a glimmer in
the eyes

The swivel of the hips

The swirl of the hair

The poetry of the soul

The stillness of the
presence

We who are lovers

We recognize each
other

I do not long

For wealth or gold

Fame or fortune

The only longing that
remains

Is to return again and
again

To the sweet dissolve

Of Love's pure presence

In the center of my
heart

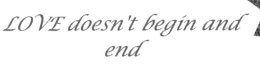

LOVE doesn't begin and
end

IT always IS

WE open and close

WE step into and out of
the river

LOVE remains as
constant

As the present moment

Always there, and
waiting

For our full
participation

And engagement

My body does not use
words to speak

Its language is the
syntax of my hips

The rhyme of my spine

The prose of my toes

The sounds of my
breath

The articulation of my
thighs

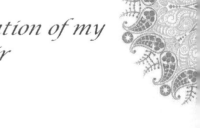

The conversation of my
hair

Continued...

The exclamations of my
passion

The discourse of my
sighs

The slang of my swing

The eloquence of my
tears

When love seizes me

Like a raging wildfire

It is LOVE'S command
itself

That I surrender and be
consumed

Who am I

To refuse

LOVE'S command?

I surrender

There is a longing
So Holy

A hunger
So deep

It makes each fine hair
on the body
Stand on end

A hunger to know
oneself

As unspeakable,
unutterable
LOVE itself

Continued...

Not a something "out
there"
But an unbearable
longing
For ONESELF

The unfathomable
LOVE
That one IS

This hunger fuels itself
Until we are ablaze
In our own
incomprehensible
beauty

Take me down to the
river
On a warm breezy day

Let me shed the cloak
Of my clothes

Lay yourself down
Upon the reeds of grace

I will beguile you
With the Goddess dance

There, by the river's
edge
I will take you on the
wings
Of Aphrodite's breasts

To a land no mortal
man hath seen

Continued...

The secret place
Where the Goddess reveals
Her secret magic

Where rituals are
performed

For her God, her Lover,
her Beloved

No one dare speak
Of these sacred secret
rituals

For the man never
returns
To the name he knew

He belongs to LOVE
itself
Forevermore

Continued...

Betrothed in the sacred
rivers of her desires
He wants nothing more

He knows he has
glimpsed
The unfathomable
mysteries
And cannot return
To the world he once
knew

He slides inside her,
and surrenders his
name forevermore

I want to be where Life
is really happening

Where it's real and raw
and naked and
undisguised

Show me your original
face

Give me your original
name

Perhaps I have gone
mad
With the love of you

Like Mirabai

There is nothing else
I need in return

Loving you in itself
Is my reward

My very breath exists
To bow, to praise, to
worship
And to love you

*You came to me
In my dreams last
night*

Naked and emptied

*From your sacrificial
devotion*

*I cradled you in my
arms
Stroked your forehead
And sang you sweet
lullabies*

Like a flower

A matured ripened
woman

In her prime

Unfurls her petals

And opens herself fully
to Life

There is a kind of LOVE

That has claimed me

Greater than any one
person

Any one God

Even any one religion

I surrender

You are my Guru

My Beloved

My Lover

And my Muse

There are many ways

To bow and praise

When the Love

From my hands

Finally placed itself

Upon my own heart

It was then I knew

I was finally home

It has simply become
thusly

Every breath I take

Every blink of my eyes

Every beat of my heart

Has become a love song
to you

Hidden inside

My secret chambers

Are etched

The ancient mysteries

Like the thousands year
old carvings

Of the Elephanta caves
in India

Awaiting your
excavation

Come...come to me my
love

All the mysteries shall
be revealed

I am not impressed by
what car you drive
How big your house is
Or even what your
titles and degrees are

What matters to me is
Can you stay looking
me in the eyes
While we are making
love

When your friends are
suffering
Do you go to them

When there is tragedy
in the world
Do you let your heart
break

Continued...

Can you find
compassion, empathy,
and forgiveness
For those who have
harmed you
Including yourself

Does it matter to you
To ease the suffering of
others
Including those you
don't know
And may never be
praised by

Can you look into the
eyes of the dying
Without flinching

Continued...

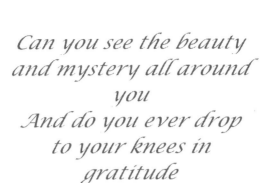

Can you see the beauty
and mystery all around
you
And do you ever drop
to your knees in
gratitude

At the unbearable
wonder and awe of it
all

Do you allow life to
break you open

Do you laugh often,
love fully, and cry
freely

Can you dance or pray

Until YOU have
dissolved

And all that is left is
LOVE

There is nothing left for
me to do

But to love you

With each and every
breath

And when at last

My last breath ceases

Even then I will love
you still

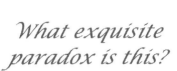

What exquisite
paradox is this?

The more I love you

The more I yearn to
love you

The more filled I am by
you

The more I ache to be
filled by you

The deeper I surrender

The more I hunger

To surrender even still

*I only had to kiss you
once*

*To ignite the eternal
flame*

That continues to blaze

In my soul

You come to me nightly
now

In my dreams

Bearing gifts

How can that be

I am already so filled

With your Love when
awake!

To get lost in your eyes

Is my greatest pleasure

To find new ways of
loving you daily

My deepest hunger

No matter what

No matter when

No matter where

I am always loving you

It will always be

Your face I see

And your name

I hear whispered

When first I wake

And before I sleep

Sometimes the worship

Inside my soul

Is so great

I cannot dance

Wildly enough

Nor kneel down low
enough

To pray

What exquisite Grace

Has brought me

To this sublime
moment?

By what name

Do I call myself now?

It is to my own hungers

That I pray

Deep within my womb

I pray and I kneel

In an instant

It was clear

I am both

The Lover

And the Loved

Since I learned

He longs for Me

Longing for Him

Never leaves me

Not even for an instant

You are my muse

The divine womb

From which

My holy longing

Is born

The fire of my longing

Is erupting

Burst me open

And bring me home

With closed eyes

I imagine

Your face

And I am sent

Into Love's rapture

From the moment

I gazed

Into your eyes

I have not

Been the same

I fell into

An infinite universe

From which

I have never returned

Play your flute for me

All night long

I will dissolve

A little more

To each strain

Of your beautiful music

Take my musky earth

Wrap your aching
around me

I'll surrender the place
within me

Where your hunger
finds its home

In whispered silences

I speak

Your name

I wandered for so long

My Beloved

Searching for you

*Only when I stopped to
rest*

Did I find you

*Waiting for me right
here*

*In the stillness of my
own heart*

You came to me again

In my dreams last night

My Beloved

Reminding me

This sweet union exists

And always has

Within me

Sometimes

"Thank You"

Is all there is

Even though I walk
alone

Dear Lord

Help me to remember

It is you

Who guides my steps

And shows me the way

There is an aching for
you

My Beloved

As the whirling dervish

Longs for God

It is because you took
up residence

Here in my heart

So long ago

That I recognize

Your footprints

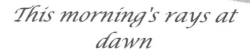

This morning's rays at
dawn

Lifted themselves up
above the mountains

And found me sitting
meditating at the
ocean's ebb

They entered my body
like liquid LOVE

Penetrated their way
down into the hidden
chambers of my secret
desires, hungers and
longings

In their warm embrace,
God made Love to me

Continued...

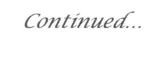

*Reaching into my cells,
my tissues, my bones,
my flesh*

*Leaving me like a
satiated lover*

*Delirious in LOVE'S
embrace*

Needing nothing

Wanting more

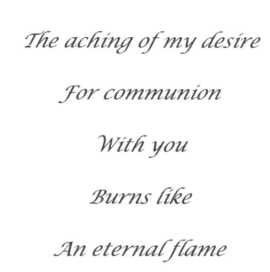

The aching of my desire

For communion

With you

Burns like

An eternal flame

Where Eros

And Love

And Poetry

And Passion

And Devotion

And Worship

And Beauty

And Surrender

Find their meeting place

There you will find me

There is a kind of love

That exists

Outside of time

And space

Outside of right

And wrong

Held hostage

By no rules

No laws

No governances

Continued...

The heart commands its ways

And the body obeys

It is a choice-less choice

All a lover can do

Is surrender and bow

Surrender and bow

Surrender and bow

I want to fan the flames

Of this longing

To breathe hot breath

Into the center of my
belly

To open myself wide
open

The yearning for YOU

The unbearable illusion

Of our separateness

The ecstatic
remembering

The wholly holy longing

Of my desire

I was doing a seemingly

Mundane task

This morning

Folding laundry

I was seized

By gratitude

For my life

Just as it is

Blessed be

My precious life

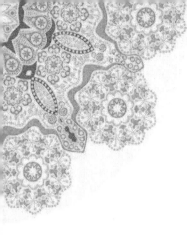

IMPREGNATED BY LOVE

A seed lay waiting

Dormant inside my
soul

You came

Whispered your name
there

Fertilizing me

Impregnating me

With your breath

That seed is blossoming
now

With glistening petals

Continued...

Unfolding

An endless unfolding

Infinity of petals

And I

I beg to offer each one

There was a time

Not long ago

When I wandered lost

Looking for you

I traveled across many
lands

Searching in temples
and shrines

Aching for you

How is it that I find
you here now

Embodied in my every
breath

Where I am never
separate from you

And never really was

I cannot say

It is "I" that loves

Or

It is "I" that prays

Love is WHAT I AM

And a prayer is WHAT
I AM

It is an effortless being
of what I AM

SHE

The mysterious,
wonderful, origins of all

SHE

The dark, wet, womb of
creation

SHE

The source of life and
creativity

Shakti

I do not know nectar
sweeter

Than the moment

Your eyes meet mine

All falseness drops
away

There we are

Nakedly exposed

Soul to soul

Love to love

The vast silence and
stillness

Beckons my soul
inward

Ever more deeply

In that unfathomable
infinite space

I AM

*I want nothing more
from my life*

*Than for my very
living itself*

*To be a sacred holy
offering*

Take my life

*And let me by thy holy
name*

Thy holy consecration

Thy holy communion

I am but an altar now

Upon which I pray

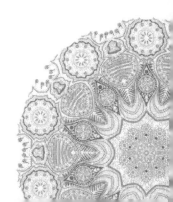

Inside the cave

Of my being

There is an altar

I worship you there

I have lost myself

In the liquid love

Of your eyes

A sweetness greater

Than wine

Today I danced

Until I lost myself

And found you

Had I only known

It was your breath

Whispering my name

All along

LOVE

It keeps calling me home

Keeps calling me home

Keeps calling me home

Love is making me

In each moment

With each breath

Love is making me

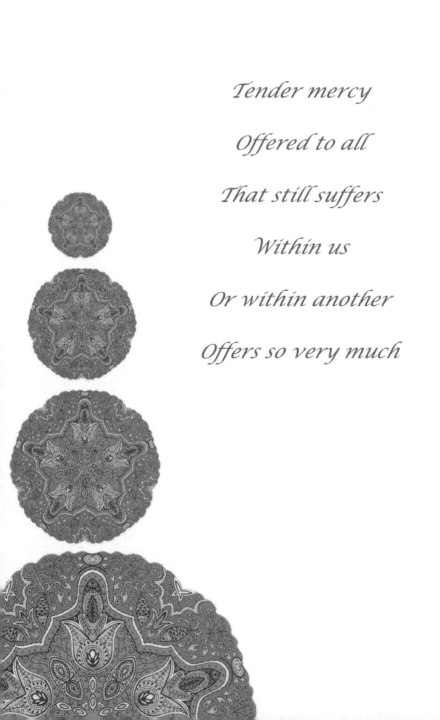

Tender mercy

Offered to all

That still suffers

Within us

Or within another

Offers so very much

Loving you

Is my daily prayer

Before I brush my teeth

I bow to pray

How much longer

Am I to bear the sound

Of your music

Beckoning me

Before I am to see

Your beautiful

Face?

Pillage and plunder me

My Love

I ache to give away

This sweet Amrita

Drink

Drink my Love

Until you are satiated

And I am emptied

Let me kiss thy lips

My Beloved

There is where

My nectar lives

My devotion

To you

Makes me

An ecstatic servant

And devotee

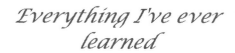

Everything I've ever
learned

At an ashram

At the feet of a guru

On my pillow

While whirling

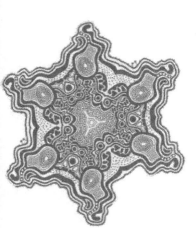

Chanting

Making love

Or bowing to pray

I have learned more

By the daily practices

Of loving my family

Continued...

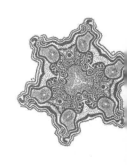

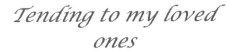

Tending to my loved ones

Caring for my neighbors

And finding kindness in my heart

In the midst of hurt and discord

Continued...

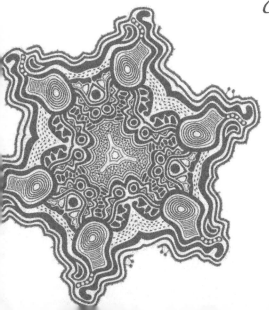

Life itself becomes the guru

Love itself becomes the teaching

The practice

The question

And the answer

A year ago today

A string got pulled

Unraveling everything

I believed myself to be

What a fucking relief

Part Two

Bonus Meanderings

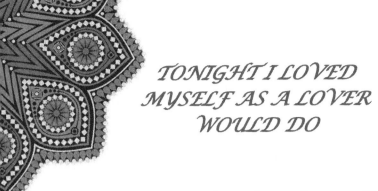

TONIGHT I LOVED MYSELF AS A LOVER WOULD DO

Tonight I loved myself
As a lover would do

With all the burning
desire, devotion and
worship
That I have ever
offered to a lover or my
Lord
Or the deities on my
altars

I bowed to myself

With all the tenderness
of a lover
I stroked and caressed
my own face

Continued...

With the watery eyes of
a lover
I beheld my own beauty

With the kindness and
admiration of a lover
I admired myself

And with the tears of a
lover
Grateful to have found
their true love
I wept

THE UNBIDDEN
HOLY RAPTURE

It comes when your
eyes become waves of
orgasms on the inside

Waves of golden elixir
rain down from the
hair follicles on the
inside of your skull
bathing you down to
your toes in wave upon
wave of golden Amrita

You can barely look out
for everything you see
is incomprehensibly
beautiful

Continued...

You realize you could
love everyone and, in
fact, you do

You've fallen to your
knees and have nothing
left you are clinging to

Nothing left to prove

You've spent your years
sitting on your zafu

Or whirling around a
million dance floors

Or felt your tears fall
upon the feet of your
guru

You've traveled up the
Himalayas

Continued...

And journeyed with
holy men

Prayed in every holy
shrine you could find

Emptied your tears and
howled at the sea

Then, it happens

You've stopped trying

Forgotten to
pray...stopped
efforting...forgotten all
about the grand Search

And suddenly, the
golden elixir starts to
rain down inside
you...unabated...
unbidden

And there you are

THE SECRET

Here's the secret

God is in the moments

We all know the
grandeur of a sunset

Or witnessing the
miracle of a birth

But God is also found in
the simplest of moments

When, in a moment of
discord,

You look into your
lover's eyes

And feel a softening

Continued...

And suddenly hope
replaces hopelessness

When, driving down
the freeway,

Absorbed in thoughts of
your To-Do list,

You glimpse a bird in
flight

And are suddenly
transported

To a state of Grace

When, walking down a
busy city street,

You are unexpectedly
accosted

Continued...

By the beauty of a rose
in full bloom

And, despite being late
for your next
appointment,

You MUST stop and
breathe in its sweet
elixir

When, walking with
your young child,

You feel the tenderness
of their tiny hand

Reach up to hold yours

And a river of warmth

Continued...

Floods your entire body

When you glimpse the nape
of your child's neck
And the swirly curl of fuzz
there

Breaks your heart wide
open

Or the crook behind
your lover's knee

Is more than you can
bear

When you lay down at
the end of your day

Continued...

*Having accomplished
nothing particularly
extraordinary*

*And find your hands
placed on your own
heart*

*And realize you are
more than okay*

More than enough

These are the moments

When God reveals itself

THE SACRED TEMPLE IN THE CENTER OF YOUR OWN BEING

There is a sacred temple
at the center of your
being

A holy sanctuary
waiting just for you

Here, there is kindness
when the world has
grown too harsh

Here, there are answers
when you have lost
your way

Here, there is
forgiveness, mercy, and
compassion
for your transgressions

Continued...

Here, there is stillness
when the world feels
chaotic and out of
control

Here, there is patience
And deep trust in your
ability to find your
way

Here, there is grace
And a cherishing so
deep you can only drop
to your knees and bow

Here, at the center of
your being is the refuge
you have wandered the
world seeking

Come...drink from this
well...drink often...drink
deeply...come...drink

LET ME ALSO SAY THIS

Longing BURNS...and
not the nice, sweet, like-
a-candle-burning-on-a-
romantic-evening kind
of burn

But the kind of burning
that can throw you into
despair, make you jump
off a bridge, have you
tearing at the sheets in
the middle of the night

For what you want but
don't have, may never
have, touched once but
lost

Continued...

When you long for a
lover but there is no
one there...when you
ache for a God you're
not even sure you
believe in
anymore...when you
are grasping to
remember what you
keep forgetting

And in those moments,
platitudes like, "trust
the moment," or advice
to Zen your way into
non-desire makes you
homicidal

This kind of longing
burns a hole in your
being, singes the hair
right off your skin,
leaves you raw, open,
defenseless

Continued...

Longing isn't just a choir singing; it's what you are willing to do when the world has gone silent and you are desperate for sound

It's what you do when you're on your hands and knees begging for mercy...for a kindness that can reach you down in the cracks where you have gone to hide because the world has gotten to feeling too harsh or too lonely or too unforgiving or too unkind

Longing like this burns you through to the other side...and it's messy and it feels like you can't bear it

Continued...

Anything else is better...getting lost in drugs, T.V., shopping, technology, gambling, sex, work, ANYTHING but feeling THIS

So what do you do? You surrender...with absolutely no guarantee that anything or anyone will come

You get down on your bloodied knees and hands that are raw from scratching at the hard earth, and you put your forehead to the ground, and you surrender

And then you surrender yet again, even more

THE INNER MARRIAGE AND THE FIRE OF LONGING

If we can burn in the flames of our longing for a Beloved, without dissolving into a relationship with an outer lover, or cutting ourselves off from the longing, a most miraculous thing begins to occur

In the unbearable crucible of our longing, one becomes both the seeker and the sought...the one longing, and the one being longed for

Continued...

Shiva and Shakti find each other in the bridal chamber of our own heart, born out of bearing the intolerable tension of our longing

Rather than relinquishing our desire, as some spiritual paths would advise, the Bhakti path seeks to fan the flames of our longing, as the great poets Rumi, Rilke, Hafiz, and others have done

These aching love poems to an imagined distant beloved, at once bring the Beloved home

Continued...

For we cannot long for
that which does not
already reside within us

It is the One you are
seeking who is seeking you

THE GLORY OF BEING A WOMAN

To writhe in sensual
pleasure

At our lover's touch

To carry the
unfathomable mystery
of Life

In our wombs

To feel the anguish of
every mother

Who has lost a child

To share the triumph of
every mother

As her baby takes its
first step

Continued...

Graduates school

Flies away

To laugh

With complete abandon

Love

Without reservation

Dance

Like the gorgeous
goddess

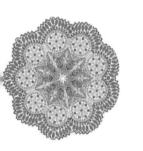

And temple dancers

We are

I LOVE being

In a woman's body

Continued...

To cry, laugh, love,
dance

In a woman's body

Today
As on all other days

I stand
In deep and profound
honor

And sisterhood

With my fellow sisters

Mothers

Daughters

Grandmothers

Granddaughters

Lovers
And friends

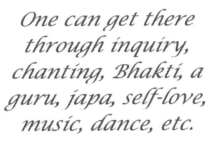

All paths hopefully lead
to the dissolution of
identification with the
self, and greater
awareness of our
Divine Self

One can get there
through inquiry,
chanting, Bhakti, a
guru, japa, self-love,
music, dance, etc.

There are many deities,
many religions, and
many paths. At the
Gnostic core of them all,
they are pointing to the
same place.

Continued...

There is nothing gained by diminishing another person's path, and everything to be gained

by contributing our collective wisdom to the very human desire and need to find our way "home."

WHAT LOVE CAN AND CANNOT REALISTICALLY DELIVER

So many love songs, poems, movies, books, promising the alluring seduction of, "You complete me."

So many tender, lonely hearts desperately seeking someone to fill the aching emptiness

Being loved by another can never fill the desperate, aching aloneness

Continued...

What love can do is
offer companionship as
we greet our own lonely
places

A loving hand placed
on our heart as we face
the darkest places

A faith in our ability to
find our way

A shared wonder at
this glorious mystery
we call being alive

A sacred sex that
reminds us that life and
love are so very, very
holy

Continued...

But love cannot make
us feel whole if we feel
un-whole

It cannot fill us up if we
feel empty

It cannot make us feel
beautiful, worthy, and
lovable, if we feel ugly
and undeserving

What love can do is
bear witness as we find
our way home...offer
shelter when the storms
are raging inside and
out...offer tenderness
when we are frightened
of the dark...dance with
us when we find our
way to the light

Continued...

If you have been failed by love's false promises...GOOD!

Let that bitter disappointment turn you toward the greatest love awaiting you inside your own beautiful and magnificent loving heart

There you will find the deepest fulfillment of love's truest promise...right there in the very center of your own glorious heart

The deepest love you have been longing for your whole life will find you there

KEEPING PERSPECTIVE

It may seem, when the nightly news is filled with yet another terrorist bombing or senseless mass shooting, that the world is, "going to hell in a hand basket."

But let's keep things in perspective

For every terrorist or mass shooter, there are hundreds, if not thousands more of us, all around the globe, who work for peace

Continued...

We are the silent
warriors that never
make the headlines

The millions upon
millions of us who,
every day, chant, pray,
do random acts of
kindness, serve the
poor, fight for equal
rights, labor in our
sadhana to become
more humble and
compassionate beings

We far outnumber
those who seek
destruction

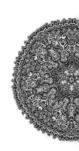

Continued...

When the news is
overwhelming
remember, that for
each terrorist that
brought down the Twin
Towers, there were
hundreds more who

rushed into the burning
buildings to save lives,
hundreds more who
opened their homes to
those who couldn't get
home, hundreds in

Canada alone who
sheltered and fed the
many people who found
themselves grounded
there that day

Continued...

For each terrorist that plotted the horrors in Paris, thousands more immediately sprung into action posting "Open Door" messages on social media, opening their homes to strangers who were abandoned on city streets as the transit systems shut down

The terrorists are a formidable foe, but we are greater, and stronger in numbers, than they will ever be. Most of humanity still wants peace

We don't make the evening news
We are silently sitting on our zafu, or joined together in meditation circles, or chanting

Continued...

Kirtan; seeking to be
peaceful, loving people

Carl Jung said that
each one of us who does
our own healing work
are, "Temple Builders."
Each awakened being
adds their brick to the
collective "temple." It is
a radical form of
activism

Each awakened heart
silently builds the
temple...and slowly the
temple is emerging

Have heart...there are
millions of us temple
builders around the
world...millions and
millions and millions

CALLING ON ALL PEACE-LOVING PEOPLE

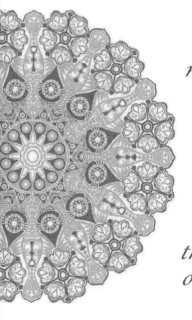

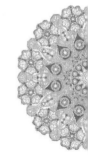

Listening to my clients this week, after weeks of devastating and seemingly endless violence in the world

I am hearing rage, despair, resignation, hopelessness, calls to action...gun control, more funding for mental health...attacks on both sides of the political divide

The rancor, fighting, pointing of fingers, blame, feels like it is threatening to fracture our human family into splinters and shards

Continued...

I don't claim to have
answers, and I am not
making a political
statement here

I am asking all of us
who want peace to
deepen our personal
practices

To drop into the very
deepest places of
wisdom and stillness

To pray for answers
that can only come
from the unified fields
of love and wholeness

To wait before we act,
until the action rises
from the deepest source
of wisdom

Continued...

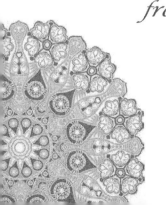

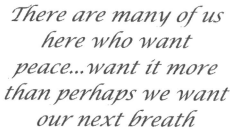

*Resist the impulse to
react until our
reactions are informed
from the very belly of
our hurting planet*

*There are many of us
here who want
peace...want it more
than perhaps we want
our next breath*

*Many of us who want
to be part of the
solution NOW...who are
tired of impotent
politicians*

*Deepen your
practice...descend to the
breath inside the
breath...wait until
wisdom from Source
rises up*

Continued...

Gandhi toppled an
entire British empire,
but he took no action
before sitting to pray
and meditate

This imbalance in OUR
world can only be
righted by each of us
dropping into the space
of peace inside our own
hearts

Nothing changes until
we do

Take the rage, grief,
heartbreak,
hopelessness, despair,
helplessness and plant
them as seeds in the
center of your heart

Continued...

Water your fervent prayers for peace there, in the center of your heart...let your tears pour onto the desecrated land of our shared anguish

Peace will be begin to grow right there on the graveyards

PEACE WILL BEGIN TO GROW

THE FINAL FRONTIER

After we have spent a
lifetime

Going out to fight our
wars

Slaying our dragons

Proving ourselves

Fighting against it all

And fighting against
ourselves

I do believe the Final
Frontier

Is when we round the
bend back home again

Continued...

To stand before
ourselves naked

War-weary, battle-
scarred, and declare

"The War Is Finally
Over!"

"I surrender...I lay
down my arms

Take off the
shield...declare a
truce..."

When we can finally
behold our own
reflection and say,

"Welcome Home"

HOW TO EXPLAIN THIS MYSTERY?

Walking through a park in India, I saw a large group of Guajarati women gathering on a bridge above me

Something about them compelled me beyond reason

I waved to them and smiled, they waved and smiled back and then walked on

Walking out of the park, I was surprised and delighted to find them walking toward me

Continued...

I don't know what compelled me, but I suddenly swung my arms wide open and ran toward them

Miraculously, they all swung their arms wide open and received me in their embrace

All I could do was weep...all they could do was weep

We touched each other's faces as one would touch the face of a Beloved one has not seen for too long

We laughed, we cried, we touched, we hugged, we held each other in

Continued...

deep and tender
wordless embrace

What could possibly
explain this mystery
This deeply feminine
knowing?

Recognition...
sisterhood...
daughterhood...
motherhood...
granddaughterhood?

If I have ever in my life
doubted that I am held
and loved
I could no longer doubt

There, in that wordless
embrace

I was more home than I
have ever been

IN HONOR OF AGING

As another year of my
life rounds the bend
I ponder my aging

It is most likely more
than half of my life
has already been lived

I have had brilliant
successes
and equally brilliant
failures

Sometimes the reality
of my increasingly
impending mortality
slices through me like a
white-hot poker knife

Continued...

And sometimes it is a
sweet and seasoned
settling
Into my wisdom years

This much I know:

I know I know less than
I used to think I knew

I trust more in the
quiet wisdom that
reaches up from the
depths within me

I cherish life more

I treasure the people I
love more

I feel more urgency
every day

Continued...

To say the things I still
need to say
And do the things I still
feel called to do

There is more need for
stillness, silence, and
solitude than there ever
was

I am softer around the
edges...all my edges

And it's easier to
maneuver in life like
this

I have found a way to
hold love in my heart

Even for the people who
have hurt me

Continued...

I am still passionate,
daring, bold, and
courageous, and
miraculously,

all the falling on my
face over the years has
not lessened that in any
way

My friends are the
wind beneath my wings

I get closer to myself
with each passing year

I think that makes me a
more interesting
human being

And everything I learn,
I have to give away

I have to make of my
life a sacred offering
Always

HE ASKED ME WHAT LOVE MEANS

He asked me what
LOVE means

And I replied

"My heart is a garden I
have been carefully
tending alone.

It is lush, and beautiful,
and wild.

You are like sunshine
pouring down upon my
garden

And even though it was
already beautiful,
bountiful,
and blooming,

Continued...

Your sunshine makes it just that much more vibrant and alive.

My blossoms are more vivid
My flowers stand taller and more erect on their stems
Everything in the garden leans towards your sun
Eager to be bathed in its warm, radiant glow."

Continued...

To which he responded,
"And your receptivity
makes my sun burn
that much brighter"

And so it could go...on,
and on, and on, and on

That, we concluded,
was as good a definition
as any

DESCENDING KUNDALINI

Sudden endless
convulsive waves
of liquid golden light

Bursting from within
the crown of my head

Flowing down like a
warm honeyed river
throughout my body

Semen-Amrita
squirting down
the back of my throat

Shiva and Shakti
cavorting like wild
lovers
in this sacred holy
bedchamber
inside my heart

We all know the
moment of conception
as an unfathomable
mystery

But what about
conception
as an internal mystery?

When years, lifetimes
perhaps,
of wanting and
waiting,
in the fermentation of
the fluids of our own
longing,
are finally penetrated
by the internal seed
of our own creative life
force?

Continued...

When Shiva from
within
penetrates and merges
with the waiting
Shakti?

Oh Glory...Oh Holy
Glory
This pregnancy is
indeed the Divine Birth
The Holy Communion

And the wafer and the
wine
That flows from this
Holy Union
The sweetest Amrita
I have ever known

TRUTH

Do not idealize me as a
saint
Nor demonize me as a
sinner,
For I am both

I am capable of
extreme acts
Of selfless generosity
But I can also be stingy

Have been exceedingly
kind
But also harsh
And sometimes cruel

Forgiving and
unforgiving

Faithful and despairing

Continued...

Deeply connected to
Source

And achingly
disconnected and adrift

Trusting and
mistrustful

Brave and terrified

Noble and cowardly

Certain and uncertain

Faithful and disloyal

Committed and
uncommitted

Continued...

Blisteringly truthful
and a liar

Open-hearted and
closed

Sincere and insincere

Knowing and clueless

Know me as I actually
am

Not who I pretend to be

NUMBERED DAYS

I know my days

On this glorious,
wondrous journey

Are numbered

Each new day

A blessing

More precious then the
last

In whatever remaining
time

May be granted to me

I want to LIVE

When I look into your
eyes

Continued...

I want to really see you

And to have you really see me

I want to see the vivid colors

Of Autumn's leaves

And wild blue skies

*To feel the sweet caress of sun
And wind upon my skin*

To cherish the sounds of children laughing

Birds singing

Continued...

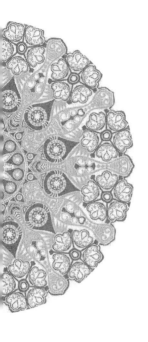

And lovers loving

I want you to know

That you are loved

Cherished

And that you matter

I want to have left
A gentle and loving
handprint

Upon your heart

And when, at last, I am
taken back

Continued...

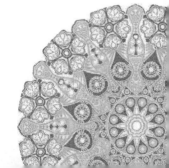

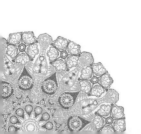

Into that unfathomable
place

Of no beginnings and
endings

May I have tread
lightly

Upon this Grand
Mystery

Leaving only love,
beauty, and grace

In my wake

HOW MY BODY SPEAKS

Solid, deep, slow,
balanced, spinning
Moving around an orb
Planted deep beyond
The center of all things

Swirling, twirling,
breathing
No head
Hair wild, body wild,
spirit wild

Nowhere, everywhere
Efforting, no effort
Finding it, losing it,
wanting to find it
again

Continued...

Staying in the dance
No matter what

Being clumsy, being
trying
Falling into it, losing
myself into it, losing it
again
Keep moving, keep
releasing, keep
breathing
Finding the thread that
weaves its way
Down the center of the
core

Out through my arms,
out through my breath
Through every strand
of hair
Through my eyelashes
and eyebrows

Continued...

And fingertips and
pores
And out my body in
every bead of sweat
A single thread pulsing

Letting my body have
fun
Letting my body know
what it loves
And love what it knows
And do what it loves

Letting my body dance
its own dance
Feel its own pleasure
Seek its own truth
Celebrate its own self

Continued...

Subtle and bold,
big and small

And all around and
nowhere

Only right here

So beautiful my heart
breaking open
Splitting into pieces
A singular soulful voice
Singing its yearning,
its love
Its remembering and
its forgetting

A sweet ecstatic aching

WHAT WOULD WE DO?

What would we do if the Buddha walked in the room, right here, right now?

Would we recognize him?

Or would we see his big, round belly and think, "That is a fat man, a man of no discipline, a weak man?"

What if Christ walked in the room?

Would we recognize him?

Continued...

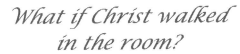

Or would we see his
wounds and think,
"There is a martyr; a man of
no self-esteem or self-worth?"

And what if Gandhi walked
in the room right here, right
now?

Would we recognize
him?

Or would we see a poor
man and rush in with
our need to help him, to
save him, to make him
"better?"

Or what about
Aphrodite?

Continued...

Would we recognize
her? Or would we say,
"She is a whore, a slut?"

Or perhaps Kali?

Would we recognize
her?

Or would we send her
to an Anger
Management class?

With what eyes would
we have to be seeing

To see the holy behind
the surface?

With what heart would
we have to be feeling

Continued...

To see the soul behind
the psychology?

With what
transparency would we
have to be embodying

To behold the saint
within the sinner?

The mystery behind the
ordinary?

What if Buddha really
is in this room right
here, right now?

And Christ? And
Gandhi? And
Aphrodite? And Kali?

Continued...

*And so many, many,
many more?*

*Would we have the eyes
to see them, the hearts
to receive them, and
the wisdom to embrace
them?*

*And if I were Radha, or
Sita, or Parvati, or
Saraswati...would you
recognize me?*

I recognize you

LOVE AND YEARNING YEARNING AND LOVE

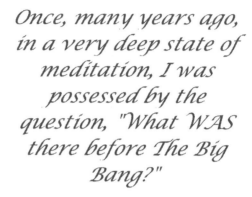

Once, many years ago, in a very deep state of meditation, I was possessed by the question, "What WAS there before The Big Bang?"

After being taken in my meditation to the bottom of a very deep spiraled cavern with hundreds of chanting Tibetan monks lining the spiral way, I was shot up as if on a spire through the opening of

Continued...

*the mountain until I
was sitting above a
vast plain*

*And there I heard God's
booming voice say, "All
there ever was, was
LOVE AND
YEARNING...
YEARNING AND
LOVE."*

A DAY AT THE BEACH WITH 300 12-YEAR OLDS: AN EROS MYSTERY PLAY

At the beach today with my daughter's school celebrating the end of 6th grade

So much on the verge of blossoming

Girls...some with barely newly budding breasts...still unselfconscious in their bodies

Others with already full breasts and hips

Continued...

Some already self
consciously hiding their
bikinied bodies behind
towels

Others flirtatiously
prancing hoping to get
someone's attention

Boys...digging holes,
throwing footballs,
playing tag

While others walk
around in sunglasses
and a forced air of
swag

Mostly girls with girls
and boys with boys, but
for the few loners
playing with sand or
hidden behind the trees

Continued...

They don't know they
are a breath away from
all of this changing

Soon there will be tidal
waves moving through
their bodies and urges
and impulses they
won't understand

This may be the last
time they spend on the
beach self-sequestered
in gendered groups

By this time next year
curiosity about the
"other" will be calling
or, for some, curiosity
about the "same" that is
different than now
What will they do with
those feelings?

Continued...

I can feel the pulsing
potency of all these
beautiful kids
on the brink of some of
life's greatest mysteries

And they still so
unawares

I know that soon, my
daughter will be "gone"
to me in some ways for
the next few years

Friends, and music, and
secret explorations will
soon replace snuggle
time

I also know she will
come back to me in
time...seasoned,
different

Continued...

*Hopefully she will come
to me with her
questions as her body
changes, her confusions
as her emotions change,
her fears or
heartbreaks or crushes
or...*

*But today, I simply
reveled in the still
innocent beauty of this
divine mystery play*

I was watching a dance
performance
of a young man with a
severe stutter

When asked why he
dances he said,
"To speak...freely."

Find your way to speak

Whether through your
voice, your dance, your
poetry, your art, your
worship, your chanting,
your loving, your
prayer

Find your way to speak

Freely

FREEDOM

There is a kind of
freedom that has slowly
emerged as I've grown
older, wiser, and my
practices have
deepened

Freedom to own my
own passions and
desires
without shame or
apology

Freedom to embrace,
love and accept, who I
am
Exactly the way I am,
In the body I am in

Freedom to make love
wholly and holy
With my whole SELF

Continued...

Mind, body, soul, and
spirit fully engaged

Freedom to pray and
worship and surrender
Until "I" dissolve fully

Freedom to express
myself directly
With kindness and
honesty
Without apology

Freedom to dance
With full and complete
abandon

Freedom to say, "No"
sometimes
And protect and
preserve my need
For silence and solitude

Continued...

Freedom to drop deeper
and deeper
Into the still pool
Of my own
unfathomable infinite
being
With less resistance

Freedom to cry easily
When Life touches me
deeply
Which it does do more
and more often

Freedom to laugh until I
snort
Without embarrassment

Freedom to love without
restraint
And without need or
demand

Continued...

For anything in return

Freedom to say, "YES"

To the subtle
whisperings
That beckon me ever
more deeply
Toward my own
unfolding

Freedom

Blessed Be

Blessed Be

LOVE BEYOND PSYCHOLOGY

There is a kind of love,
and loving, beyond the
fear of "unhelpful
dependencies"

Outside the psychology
paradigm entirely

Where surrendering is
not losing oneself

Or giving oneself away

Or giving something up

It is a matter of
claiming one's
birthright

To claim back that
WHAT I AM IS LOVE

Continued...

In the act of
surrendering myself TO
IT, I am redeemed

We are redeemed

Love itself is redeemed

There is no fear in this
space

The matter of
"unhelpful
dependencies" is
irrelevant

It is so far beyond that

There is a holding-
nothing-back

A fully-letting-go that
has one enter the divine
dance of the Gods

Continued...

It is the field of "no wrongdoing and no rightdoing" that Rumi spoke of

It is the whirling dervish who begs to give his life away

What would he hold onto once he has arrived at knowing that all he is is LOVE

All there is is LOVE

All we are here for is to surrender to LOVE

Who cares who comes forward first or who doesn't

Continued...

Both people are aching
to come forward

Finding creative and
more creative and
more creative ways to
come forward

This is precisely where
love is, where it gets
offered, and where we
stand on holy ground

One could even be so
bold as to want for that
with each and every
breath

SAYING YES TO LONGING

Once, while I was
leading a tour group
through India, we
arrived at the holiest
Hindu temple in
Varanasi

Unbeknownst to me, no
Non-Hindu Indians are
allowed entry

Signs posted all around
the temple, and armed
guards enforcing it

The group wandered off
as I was suddenly
OVERCOME by a DEEP
LONGING to be inside

I tried negotiating,
pleading, flirting, even

Continued...

bribing the armed
guards, but to no avail

Rather than walking
away in utter despair
and resignation, I stood
in the doorway of that
temple, closed my eyes,
and deliberately fanned
the flames of my
longing until I lost all
sense of time and place

I was on fire in my own
longing

If I couldn't have entry
to the temple, I could at
least say, "YES" to my
own longing

Lost in this timeless and
profound reverie,

Continued...

eventually I felt
someone tapping my
shoulder

The armed guard,
seeing my deep prayer,
had gone inside the
temple, brought the
priest out to witness my
longing, and together
they silently escorted
me across the threshold
into the temple

Collapsing against the
inner wall of the
temple, sobbing tears of
gratitude, it was then
that I KNEW

My job is to say, "YES,
YES, YES" to my own
deepest longing

Continued...

*"YES" when it seems
impossible*

*"YES" when I feel
despair*

*"YES" when my heart is
breaking*

*"YES" when I no longer
believe*

"YES" no matter what

*Sooner or later, Life,
Love, God, something,
taps me on the shoulder
and carries me across
the threshold*

Continued...

Not always in the manner I wanted, or the person I imagined,

but I am ALWAYS inevitably carried into the inner sanctum...the Holy of Holies

What I have to do is keep saying, "YES" to my own Holy Longing

I do not see my job as a therapist and spiritual guide to stand behind some impersonal, clinical reserve

More than anything I ever learned in graduate school, what I find most meaningful and helpful with my clients is my hard-earned wisdom on how to navigate this oftentimes challenging and bewildering mystery called life

How to survive heartbreak, disappointment, despair, failure, loss

How to find meaning in suffering

Continued...

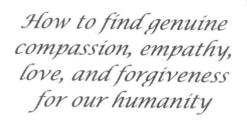

How to find genuine
compassion, empathy,
love, and forgiveness
for our humanity

How to open fully to
the mystery, wonder,
beauty, and awe all
around us at all times

How to love well, fight
fair, forgive easily, and
return again and again
and again to love

How to find the
poignancy and
immediacy of life in
each moment

I honestly learned none
of these things through
textbooks but through
the arduous and

Continued...

devoted years of my
own living

My sadhana, my
practice, my mistakes,
my awakenings, my
softenings, my countless
years of learning, and
relearning again and
again how to open
myself and my heart to
life and to love

The courage I have
forged, the resilience I
have grown, the
tenderness I have
cultivated

We are all journeyers
together on this
magical mystery tour

Continued...

What I offer is the honest and raw wisdom gained from my journey

I find it helps grateful fellow journeyers find their way through the dark

Namaste

FOR THOSE WHO CARE TO KNOW, THERE IS HOPE

I know I sound like a
madwoman gone drunk
on the elixirs of Love,
but here's what you
should know

There was a time when
I was completely
stripped down to the
bone

Asked to sacrifice so
much of who and what
I loved

There were days when I
couldn't get out of bed

Days when the despair,
grief, anguish, and loss

Continued...

felt like more than I
could bear...more than I
wanted to bear

I retreated from much
of my outer life to cry
and to grieve, to wail
and to moan, to beg
and to pray for healing
and restoration to come

More tears were shed in
one year than were
shed over the entire
rest of my life
cumulatively

There were moments
when I wasn't sure I
would make it through

When dear friends
came and sat beside me
just so I could feel
where I began and
ended

Continued...

I was stripped down naked, down to the very bones of myself

For much of the time I was resisting the stripping down

When I could resist and fight no longer, I FINALLY surrendered

When I felt completely forsaken by life, by Love, by EVERYTHING, only then did I FINALLY surrender

Only then did I begin to BEG to be stripped even further

Continued...

"Take me," I cried

"Take all of me...I give
it all up"

Only then did I enter a
place of profound
silence and stillness

Only then did an
unfathomable amount
of love and light begin
pouring into me

Only when I
surrendered totally and
completely was I able to
feel how deeply loved
by Life I always am

It wasn't until I
dropped to my knees in
complete humility that
I rediscovered yet

Continued...

again that *I AM LOVE ITSELF*

Now, I can't give this love away fast enough

All my very being wants to do is to *LOVE* with each and every breath because there is *NOTHING LEFT TO DO*

Even in the very, very darkest hours lie the seeds of light

There is always hope

Sitting with a friend
this morning as he bid
his final goodbyes to his
beloved mom; he, who is
himself on day-leave
from the hospital as he
battles bone cancer

Life can be so raw and
harsh sometimes;
snatching those we love

We, too, all in our own
time will pass from this
existence to whatever
mystery may lie ahead

It has always been, and
continues to be my
prayer to meet Life on
ITS terms

Continued...

To allow both the exquisite
agony and ecstasy
to break me open
and break me apart
and make me more whole
On its terms

To meet it all with
courage and grace

To say I LOVE YOU
often enough that no
matter what may
happen, those will have
been the last words you
ever heard me speak

I LOVE YOU

WHEN I DIE
REMEMBER ME

*Remember me for the
love I gave*

*For the friendship I
offered*

*For the tears I cried
with you*

*For my unbridled
laughter*

*For the loving arms I
offered*

*When you needed
comfort*

For the way I danced

Continued...

For the silent presence I offered

For the way I made love

For whatever wisdom I may have offered

For the courage my life may have demonstrated

For the moments of caring, kindness, compassion, empathy, and generosity I may have offered

For the little daily gestures

Continued...

And if there were moments when I failed you

Because I was lost, or hurting, or selfish, or unkind

Please forgive me

Know that loving you

Was all I ever intended to do

About The Author

Tina M. Benson, M.A., is the author of the internationally bestselling book, "*A Woman Unto Herself: A Different Kind of Love Story.*" She is a modern-day soulwhisperer and transpersonal/ Jungian-oriented spiritual teacher and life coach. With a Masters degree in counseling psychology from Lesley College Graduate School, she has more than 30 years experience, both in the United States and abroad, teaching, leading, and facilitating individuals, and couples, as well as large and small groups through consciousness explorations, chakra initiation/meditation retreats, couples and women's retreats, ecstatic dancing, Voice Dialogue, Enneagram, chanting, ritual, and travel to sacred sites around the world. She is the founder and creator of the SoulSpeaks Project, creator of the short documentary film *What Matters Most*, and is also a non-denominational ordained minister, officiating at weddings, birth, death, and other life-passages and celebrations. Tina lives and practices in Marin County, California.

Visit: www.soulwhisperer.com

Other Books By Tina M. Benson, M.A.

A Woman Unto Herself:
A Different Kind of Love Story

Available on Amazon
at
http://amzn.to/1QgWc96

46158192R00120

Made in the USA
San Bernardino, CA
27 February 2017